CHAPTER QUIZZES
FOR COON'S

PSYCHOLOGY
A JOURNEY

Sandra Madison
Delgado Community College

WADSWORTH

THOMSON LEARNING

Australia • Canada • Mexico • Singapore • Spain • United Kingdom • United States

**For more information about our products,
contact us at:
Thomson Learning Academic Resource Center
1-800-423-0563**

**For permission to use material from this text,
contact us by:
Phone: 1-800-730-2214
Fax: 1-800-731-2215
Web: www.thomsonrights.com**

Asia
Thomson Learning
60 Albert Complex, #15-01
Albert Complex
Singapore 189969

Australia
Nelson Thomson Learning
102 Dodds Street
South Street
South Melbourne, Victoria 3205
Australia

Canada
Nelson Thomson Learning
1120 Birchmount Road
Toronto, Ontario M1K 5G4
Canada

Europe/Middle East/South Africa
Thomson Learning
Berkshire House
168-173 High Holborn
London WC1 V7AA
United Kingdom

Latin America
Thomson Learning
Seneca, 53
Colonia Polanco
11560 Mexico D.F.
Mexico

Spain
Paraninfo Thomson Learning
Calle/Magallanes, 25
28015 Madrid, Spain

Table of Contents

Chapter 1: Psychology: The Search for Understanding

1.   Which of the following describes a positive correlation?
        a.   When the temperature increases, activity level decreases.
        b.   As gas prices increase, traveling decreases.
        c.   The less hair a person has, the higher his intelligence is.
        d.   As temperatures fall outside, activity levels decline.

2.   Which of the following correlation coefficients indicates the strongest relationship?
        a.   +.75
        b.   -.13
        c.   -78
        d.   .00

3.   A correlation coefficient of +1.23 indicates that:
        a.   you've made an error in computation.
        b.   you have a high positive correlation.
        c.   you can discuss causation.
        d.   you can make a prediction based on your finding.

4.   In an experiment, changes in the _____variable are attributed to changes in the
        _____ variable assuming all other conditions are held constant.
        a.   independent; dependent
        b.   dependent; independent
        c.   dependent; extraneous
        d.   experimental; independent

5.   Psychology is defined as:
        a.   the study of the mind.
        b.   the study of mental disorders.
        c.   the scientific study of unconscious motivations.
        d.   the scientific study of human and animal behavior.

6.   The first woman to earn a Ph.D. in psychology was
        a.   Mary Calkins.
        b.   Anna Freud.
        c.   Margaret Washburn.
        d.   Christine Ladd-Franklin.

7.   According to Freud, glimpses of the unconscious were revealed in everyday life through
        all of the following EXCEPT:
        a.   dreams
        b.   emotions
        c.   slips of the tongue
        d.   conscious determinants

8. Which is NOT one of the basic goals of psychology?
   a. to predict
   b. to evaluate
   c. to explain
   d. to describe

9. Which early school of psychology relied on a method called introspection?
   a. functionalism
   b. Gestalt psychology
   c. behaviorism
   d. structuralism

10. The psychologist who investigates the changes the immune system makes in behavior would most likely subscribes to the _____ perspective of psychology.
    a. humanistic
    b. cognitive
    c. biological
    d. behavioral

11. The _____ perspective of psychology focuses on how people process information, develop language, solve problems and think.
    a. cognitive
    b. biological
    c. behavioral
    d. humanistic

12. In general, _____ refers to the practice of actively questioning statements rather than blindly accepting them.
    a. critical thinking
    b. implicit thought
    c. manifest thinking
    d. explicit thought

13. Which type of research method is used to identify cause-and-effect relationships?
    a. naturalistic observation
    b. survey
    c. experimental method
    d. descriptive method

14. A _____ is an in-depth investigation of a single individual, involving information from a wide variety of sources.
    a. survey
    b. case study
    c. testimony
    d. sample

15. In an experiment, the _____ variable is affected by changes in the independent variable.
   a. independent
   b. dependent
   c. extraneous
   d. explicit

16. In an experiment, the researcher deliberately manipulates the _____ variable.
   a. independent
   b. dependent
   c. extraneous
   d. descriptive

17. The experimental group:
   a. receives the dependent variable.
   b. receives the independent variable.
   c. determines what is ethical.
   d. receives the placebo.

18. In an experiment, the _____ group is exposed to all the experimental conditions, except for the independent variable.
   a. control
   b. experimental
   c. treatment
   d. independent

19. In an experiment, when neither the experimenters nor the subject knows in which group the subject is being placed, the experimenter is using a _____ technique.
   a. single-blind
   b. double-blind
   c. random assignment
   d. replication

20. Replication of research findings
   a. is a waste of time.
   b. detracts from the validity of those findings.
   c. increases confidence in the accuracy of those findings.
   d. is called plagiarism.

Chapter 2: Brain and Behavior

1. The neuron fibers that are the primary receivers of information from other neurons are called:
    a. dendrites.
    b. soma.
    c. axons.
    d. glial cells.

2. During a(n)_____ potential the axon is said to be polarized where it is more negative inside than outside.
    a. action
    b. resting
    c. negative after-
    d. positive

3. Once an axon has been fired, a mild explosion will occur where neurotransmitters are released from the synaptic vesicles, located in the _____ terminal, into the synaptic cleft.
    a. dendrite
    b. receptor
    c. axon
    d. modulator

4. Serotonin, dopamine, acetylcholine and endorphins are all examples of:
    a. hormones.
    b. neurotransmitters.
    c. modulators.
    d. neuropeptides.

5. The brain and the spinal cord make up the _____ nervous system.
    a. peripheral
    b. somatic
    c. central
    d. autonomic

6. The _____ controls heart rate, breathing and blood pressure.
    a. medulla
    b. thalamus
    c. motor cortex
    d. cerebellum

7. The hippocampus is the part of the limbic system primarily involved in:
   a. influencing attention and arousal.
   b. relaying sensory information.
   c. coordinating complex body movements.
   d. forming memories.

8. The _____ connects the brain with the peripheral nervous system.
   a. corpus callosum
   b. spinal chord
   c. axon
   d. sympathetic branch

9. The area of the brain that serves as a relay station for sensory information flowing into the brain is known as the:
   a. cerebellum.
   b. medulla.
   c. reticular formation.
   d. thalamus.

10. The thick band of fibers that connects the two cerebral hemispheres is known as the:
    a. cerebrum.
    b. cortex.
    c. corpus callosum.
    d. glial cells.

11. Split brain surgery:
    a. is used for people suffering from severe epilepsy.
    b. does not provide a means of studying the function of the individual hemispheres.
    c. drastically changes intelligence, personality and behavior.
    d. prevents transfer of information across the synapse.

12. Which of the following reveals the electrical activity of the brain by producing a record of the brain waves?
    a. EEG
    b. CT scans
    c. Pet scan
    d. MRI

13. The _____ nervous system prepares the body during times of stress; the _____ returns the body to normal once the emergency is over.
    a. somatic; autonomic
    b. parasympathetic; sympathetic
    c. autonomic; somatic
    d. sympathetic; parasympathetic

14. During a resting state the axon:
    a. is permeable to sodium.
    b. is neither transmitting nor receiving information.
    c. is transmitting and receiving information.
    d. is depolarized.

15. The all-or-none law refers only to the:
    a. neuron.
    b. glial cells.
    c. axon.
    d. dendrites.

16. The two subdivisions of the peripheral nervous systems are the:
    a. spinal cord and brain.
    b. somatic and autonomic.
    c. sympathetic and parasympathetic.
    d. afferent and efferent.

17. The hypothalamus controls all of the following EXCEPT:
    a. hunger
    b. thirst
    c. memory
    d. body temperature

18. In the mid-1800s the accidental injury of the railroad worker named Phineas Gage provided compelling evidence of behavioral changes due to carnage of the:
    a. right cerebral hemisphere.
    b. frontal lobe.
    c. hypothalamus.
    d. hippocampus.

19. Although people with _____ aphasia can speak easily, they often have trouble understanding written or spoken language.
    a. Broca's
    b. Wernicke's
    c. limited
    d. comprehension

20. The _____have the greatest degree of representation on both the somatosensory cortex and the primary motor cortex.
    a. hands and the face
    b. arms and legs
    c. neck and torso
    d. legs and feet

Chapter 3: Human Development

1. The Russian psychologist _____ believed that private speech is a key component in a child's cognitive development.
    a. Erik Erikson
    b. Lev Vygotsky
    c. Sigmund Freud
    d. Max Wertheimer

2. Piaget believed that people pass through the cognitive stages:
    a. in different orders.
    b. at varying rates.
    c. in the same order but not at the same rate.
    d. in the same order and at same rate.

3. Two-year-old Danielle says "Mommy!" whenever she sees any woman. She uses a process Piaget called:
    a. accommodation.
    b. assimilation.
    c. private speech.
    d. conservation.

4. When four-year-old Kendra's teacher rolls a ball of clay into a sausage shape, Kendra believes the sausage has more clay than the ball. This demonstrates that she has not acquired the concept of:
    a. reversibility.
    b. contortion.
    c. object permanence.
    d. conservation.

5. Jean Piaget felt that:
    a. not all individuals reach formal operations.
    b. everyone achieves formal operations.
    c. the zone of proximal development facilitates development.
    d. development is forged within a sociocultural environment.

6. According to _____, each stage of the life span is marked by a particular conflict which can be resolved in either a psychologically positive or negative way.
    a. Erik Erikson
    b. Lawrence Kohlberg
    c. Abraham Maslow
    d. Carl Rogers

7. According to the psychosocial theory, a child entering adolescence can expect major developmental task demands to center around the need to:
    a.   trust others.
    b.   achieve intimacy.
    c.   acquire autonomy.
    d.   develop a sense of self.

8. The key psychosocial conflict confronting an elderly woman is:
    a.   generativity vs. stagnation
    b.   integrity vs. despair
    c.   trust vs. mistrust
    d.   intimacy vs. isolation

9. Change in physical, cognitive and social abilities throughout the life span is known as:
    a.   assimilation.
    b.   inheritance.
    c.   development.
    d.   conservation.

10. The debate that exists over whether or not development is due to genetics or environment is often referred to as:
    a.   heredity vs. conservation.
    b.   assimilation vs. accommodation.
    c.   nature vs. nurture.
    d.   continuity vs. discontinuity.

11. The germinal or zygote phase ends:
    a.   after birth.
    b.   approximately 28 days after conception.
    c.   once the gametes unite.
    d.   once the zygote has implanted itself into the uterus.

12. Cigarette smoking during pregnancy has been associated with which of the following problems?
    a.   large head size
    b.   premature birth and low birth weight
    c.   FAS
    d.   hyperlexia

13. Wendy was born with widely spaced eyes and flattened nose. She later developed signs of mental retardation and growth defects. These are symptoms of:
    a.   cocaine abuse.
    b.   excessive caffeine consumption.
    c.   fetal alcohol syndrome.
    d.   premature birth.

14.   During the embryonic period, the parts of the body near the head develop more quickly than the parts near the feet. This type of growth is known as:
        a.   proximidistal growth.
        b.   cephalocaudal growth.
        c.   overextension.
        d.   peripheral development.

15.   According to your text, which of the following senses is the least developed at birth?
        a.   vision
        b.   hearing
        c.   smell
        d.   touch

16.   When we change our cognitive structure to fit new stimuli we have encountered, we are using:
        a.   assimilation.
        b.   accommodation.
        c.   conservation.
        d.   reversibility.

17.   According to Piaget, the major cognitive task during the pre-operational stage is the development of:
        a.   the ability to think abstractly.
        b.   object permanence.
        c.   symbols and words.
        d.   conservation skills.

18.   Chemicals that can cause birth defects are called:
        a.   biohazards.
        b.   teratogens.
        c.   amniocentesis.
        d.   antioxidants.

19.   If two ova are released and fertilized, what will be the result?
        a.   identical twins
        b.   fraternal twins
        c.   Down's syndrome
        d.   miscarriage

20.   Kerry sees and thinks of the world from his viewpoint and has difficulty appreciating another's viewpoint. Kerry's thinking can be described as:
        a.   egotistical.
        b.   egocentric.
        c.   accommodating.
        d.   conceited.

Chapter 4: Sensation and Perception

1. Each morning when Elaine goes to work at a coffee mill, she smells the strong odor of coffee. After she's there for a few minutes, she is no longer aware of it. This is called:
    a. transduction.
    b. sensory adaptation.
    c. signal detection theory.
    d. just noticeable difference.

2. The process through which the senses detect sensory information and transmit it to the brain is called:
    a. sensation.
    b. perception.
    c. impulse.
    d. adaptation.

3. The eye changes light waves into impulses and the ear changes sound waves into impulses. These are examples of:
    a. perception.
    b. transduction.
    c. accommodation.
    d. adaptation.

4. Rods contain:
    a. opsin.
    b. rhodopsin.
    c. biopsin.
    d. chromospin.

5. The structure responsible for our ability to see color is the:
    a. cone.
    b. rod.
    c. thalamus.
    d. lens.

6. According to the trichromatic theory, the primary colors are:
    a. yellow, blue, and white.
    b. blue, green, and red.
    c. orange, green, and gray.
    d. black, brown, and white.

7.   As the decibels of a sound increases the:
     a.   frequency increases.
     b.   frequency decreases.
     c.   amplitude decreases.
     d.   amplitude increases.

8.   Vibrations are amplified in the:
     a.   outer ear.
     b.   inner ear.
     c.   middle ear.
     d.   auditory nerve.

9.   The auditory receptors are called:
     a.   hair cells.
     b.   rods.
     c.   ossicles.
     d.   cones.

10. The structures in the inner ear that helps us to maintain balance are called the:
     a.   tympanic membranes.
     b.   semi-circular canals.
     c.   ossicles.
     d.   pacinian corpuscles.

11. Cochlear implants involve small electronic devices designed to take the place of the:
     a.   outer ear.
     b.   basilar membrane.
     c.   eardrum.
     d.   hair cells.

12. The olfactory receptors are located in the:
     a.   olfactory nerve.
     b.   olfactory bulb.
     c.   olfactory canal.
     d.   olfactory membrane.

13. The principle of _____ states that we tend to fill in missing parts of a figure.
     a.   closure
     b.   simplicity
     c.   figure ground
     d.   proximity

14. According to motion parallax, near objects appear _____, where as distant objects appear:
    a.   smaller; larger.
    b.   to move quickly; to move slowly.
    c.   textured; gradient.
    d.   hazy; clear.

15. A(n) _____ is a distorted perception of reality.
    a.   interposition
    b.   motion parallax
    c.   illusion
    d.   linear reversal

16. According to the _____ theory, one type of coding system in the eye can transmit messages for red and green.
    a.   trichromatic
    b.   opponent-process
    c.   afterimage
    d.   dichromatic

17. The perceptual tendency to group together objects that are near each other is called:
    a.   nearness.
    b.   similarity.
    c.   continuity.
    d.   closure.

18. Pure tendency to perceive an object as being the same size in spite of the retinal image size is referred to as:
    a.   convergence.
    b.   retinal disparity.
    c.   color constancy.
    d.   size constancy.

19. The _____ theory states that impulses in the auditory nerve follow the pattern of the sound waves being detected.
    a.   place
    b.   pitch
    c.   frequency
    d.   timbre

20. The four qualities of taste are: sweet, sour, _____ and:
    a.   bitter; spicy.
    b.   bitter; salty.
    c.   salty; spicy.
    d.   salty; hot.

Chapter 5: States of Consciousness

1. Following REM deprivation there is usually:
   a. a decrease in REM sleep.
   b. an increase in REM sleep.
   c. absence of REM sleep.
   d. no change in REM sleep.

2. NREM dreams are:
   a. emotional.
   b. more visual.
   c. thought-like.
   d. vivid.

3. Use of _____ leads to decreased activity in the central nervous system.
   a. stimulants
   b. depressants
   c. hallucinogens
   d. psilocybin

4. Which drug category alters perception and mood leading to hallucinations?
   a. stimulants
   b. depressants
   c. narcotics
   d. hallucinogens

5. Sleepwalking and sleeptalking typically occur during:
   a. stage 1 NREM.
   b. REM sleep.
   c. stage 4 NREM.
   d. stage 2 NREM.

6. Which of the following is NOT a stimulant?
   a. cocaine
   b. caffeine
   c. nicotine
   d. alcohol

7. An episode of night terror typically takes place during:
   a. REM sleep.
   b. paradoxical sleep.
   c. stage 1 NREM.
   d. stage 4 NREM.

8. The EEG pattern when one is drowsy and ready for sleep is characterized by:
   a. alpha waves.
   b. beta waves.
   c. delta waves.
   d. sleep spindles.

9. Short bursts of brain activity in stage 2 NREM are called:
   a. delta waves.
   b. alpha waves.
   c. beta waves.
   d. sleep spindles.

10. The two most basic stages of sleep are:
    a. alpha and beta sleep.
    b. superficial and deep sleep.
    c. REM and hypnogogic sleep.
    d. REM and NREM sleep.

11. Karl suffers from sudden irresistible urges to sleep during the daytime, which can last from a few minutes to a half hour. This is called:
    a. narcolepsy.
    b. sleep apnea.
    c. somnambulism.
    d. paradoxical sleep.

12. Some physicians believe that SIDS, or crib death, may be caused by:
    a. prematurity.
    b. narcolepsy.
    c. sleep apnea.
    d. sleep spindles.

13. Which of the following cannot be obtained through hypnosis?
    a. amnesia
    b. pain relief
    c. superhuman strength
    d. sensory changes

14. _____ is a mental exercise that is used to alter consciousness allowing the subject to interrupt the typical flow of thoughts.
    a. Dreaming
    b. Meditation
    c. Mantras
    d. Transcendence

15. The use of drugs to maintain psychological comfort and well-being is called:
    a.   tolerance.
    b.   dependence.
    c.   addiction.
    d.   withdrawal.

16. Lindsay has problems going to sleep and staying asleep. Lindsay is suffering from:
    a.   paradoxical sleep.
    b.   hypnogogic sleep.
    c.   sensory depreciation.
    d.   insomnia.

17. Using your bedroom for sleeping and not for studying, paying bills, or arguing is an example of a technique for coping with insomnia called:
    a.   stimulus control.
    b.   paradoxical control.
    c.   visual imagery.
    d.   progressive relaxation.

18. A mantra would most commonly be used in:
    a.   Perls' method of dream interpretation.
    b.   sensory deprivation research.
    c.   inducing hypnosis.
    d.   concentrative meditation.

19. Which of the following is a hallucinogen?
    a.   LSD
    b.   THC
    c.   hashish
    d.   all of the above

20. Which of the following does not belong with the others?
    a.   nicotine
    b.   caffeine
    c.   cocaine
    d.   codeine

Chapter 6: Conditioning and Learning

1. According to Pavlov, the dog salivating in response to meat is a(n):
    a. conditioned response.
    b. conditioned stimulus.
    c. unconditioned response.
    d. unconditioned stimulus.

2. Essentially, classical conditioning is a process of learning:
    a. the consequence that follows the behavior.
    b. by observing others.
    c. through associations.
    d. through reinforcement and punishment.

3. A relatively permanent change in behavior resulting from experience is the definition of:
    a. learning.
    b. imprinting.
    c. extinction.
    d. generalization.

4. The researcher who formulated the law-of-effect using cats in puzzle boxes and researched trial-and-error learning is:
    a. Thorndike.
    b. Skinner.
    c. Pavlov.
    d. Watson.

5. Operant conditioning has been extensively researched by:
    a. Watson.
    b. Thorndike.
    c. Skinner.
    d. Pavlov.

6. According to Pavlov, _____ occurs when the subject responds to some stimuli, but not to others.
    a. generalization
    b. discrimination
    c. spontaneous recovery
    d. extinction

7. The unexpected reappearance of old associations or conditioned response is known as:
    a. spontaneous recovery.
    b. discrimination.
    c. generalization.
    d. extinction.

8.	_____ conditioned rats through shaping to press a lever for food.
	a.	Ivan Pavlov
	b.	B.F. Skinner
	c.	Edward Thorndike
	d.	Edward Tolman

9.	Reinforcing behavior in increments which will eventually add up to the desired behaviors is know as:
	a.	intermittent reinforcement.
	b.	negative reinforcement.
	c.	shaping.
	d.	generalization.

10.	The behavior to be learned in operant conditioning is:
	a.	reflexive.
	b.	elicited.
	c.	automatic.
	d.	voluntary.

11.	A subject is more likely to repeat a behavior in the future if the behavior is:
	a.	reinforced.
	b.	punished.
	c.	involuntary.
	d.	contingent.

12.	Which of the following is not an example of a primary reinforcer?
	a.	water
	b.	a sexual encounter
	c.	a hundred dollar bill
	d.	shelter

13.	_____ reinforcement is most effective in conditioning a new response; _____ reinforcement is best for maintaining the response.
	a.	Partial; continuous
	b.	Continuous; partial
	c.	Primary; secondary
	d.	Negative; positive

14.	Which schedule of reinforcement yields the highest rate of response and the greatest resistance to extinction?
	a.	variable ratio schedule
	b.	fixed ratio schedule
	c.	variable interval schedule
	d.	fixed interval schedule

15. For every 10 baskets Anthony makes, his coach gives him $5. Anthony is being paid on a _____ schedule of reinforcement.
    a.   fixed ratio
    b.   fixed interval
    c.   variable ratio
    d.   variable interval

16. Which of the following is NOT an example of a secondary reinforcer?
    a.   colored stickers on a chart
    b.   poker chips
    c.   a glass of water
    d.   praise

17. Which of the following theorists argued that learning could take place when someone is watching another person, and later performs that behavior even when not reinforced?
    a.   B.F. Skinner
    b.   Edward Tolman
    c.   Albert Bandura
    d.   Edward Thorndike

18. Which of the following processes occur in operant conditioning when reinforcers are withheld?
    a.   generalization
    b.   discrimination
    c.   spontaneous recovery
    d.   extinction

19. Imani was once frightened by a mouse and now is afraid of hamsters, gerbils and guinea pigs. Which response accounts for her feelings?
    a.   discrimination
    b.   generalization
    c.   extinction
    d.   spontaneous recovery

20. If the conditioned stimulus is repeatedly presented without the unconditioned stimulus what will occur?
    a.   generalization
    b.   discrimination
    c.   extinction
    d.   spontaneous recovery

Chapter 7: Memory

1. The ability to retain information over time through encoding, storage, and retrieval is known as:
    a. memory.
    b. recall.
    c. working memory.
    d. declarative memory.

2. The part of memory where information stored relatively permanently is called:
    a. sensory memory.
    b. short-term memory.
    c. long-term memory.
    d. echoic memory.

3. When information is transformed into a form that can be stored, this is called:
    a. encoding.
    b. consolidation.
    c. storage.
    d. decoding.

4. Remembering is bringing the material that has been stored to mind through a process called:
    a. encoding.
    b. retrieval.
    c. storage.
    d. decoding.

5. The memory system that has a virtually unlimited capacity and long duration is known as:
    a. long-term memory.
    b. sensory memory.
    c. short-term memory.
    d. working memory.

6. What system allows you to see your visual world as smooth and fluid rather than jerky?
    a. semantic memory
    b. short-term memory
    c. iconic memory
    d. eidetic memory

7. The form of memory that allows an individual to remember speech sounds long enough to understand words is know as:
   a. iconic memory.
   b. eidetic memory.
   c. semantic memory.
   d. echoic memory.

8. If you repeat a phone number over and over again with the hopes of remembering it, you have practiced:
   a. elaborative rehearsal.
   b. episodic rehearsal.
   c. maintenance rehearsal.
   d. chunking.

9. The capacity of short-term memory seems to be about:
   a. five items.
   b. seven items.
   c. ten items.
   d. fifteen items.

10. The amount of information that can be processed in short-term memory is typically increased through a process known as:
    a. convergence.
    b. chunking.
    c. rehearsal.
    d. recall.

11. The fact that Columbus sailed the ocean blue in 1492 is probably stored in which memory system?
    a. episodic.
    b. procedural.
    c. semantic.
    d. elaborative.

12. The ability to remember your first kiss and what you wore when it happened is made possible through _____ memory.
    a. semantic
    b. procedural
    c. episodic
    d. consequential

13. Which system of long-term memory does not require conscious awareness?
    a. episodic memory
    b. semantic memory
    c. implicit memory
    d. declarative memory

14. The _____ suggests that units of information in long-term memory be organized in a complex system of associations.
    a. serial position model
    b. congruence model
    c. semantic network model
    d. retrieval model

15. The tendency to remember items at the beginning of the list is called _____ and the tendency to remember items at the end of the list is called:
    a. recency effect; primacy effect.
    b. proactive effect; retroactive effect.
    c. retroactive effect; proactive effect.
    d. primacy effect; recency effect.

16. Which psychologist pioneered the scientific study of forgetting?
    a. Herman Ebbinghaus
    b. Karl Ashley
    c. Lawrence Kohlberg
    d. Erick Erikson

17. The graphic representation of Ebbinghaus' research is called the:
    a. learning curve.
    b. memory curve.
    c. forgetting curve.
    d. retroactive curve.

18. When old memories interfere with new memories _____ has occurred.
    a. proactive interference
    b. retroactive interference
    c. repression
    d. encoding failure

19. When new memories interfere with old memories, _____ has occurred.
    a. proactive interference
    b. repression
    c. encoding failure
    d. retroactive interference

20. Which type of forgetting did Freud coin?
    a. suppression
    b. repression
    c. decay
    d. blocking

Chapter 8: Cognition, Intelligence and Creativity

1.   The psychological process that involves manipulating mental representations of information toward some goal, purpose, or conclusion is called:
   a.   thinking.
   b.   sensation.
   c.   learning.
   d.   perception.

2.   Classifying objects on the basis of their relationship to something else is a _____ concept.
   a.   disjunctive
   b.   conjunctive
   c.   relational
   d.   abstract

3.   Most people tend to think of and identify concepts in terms of ideal models or:
   a.   conjunctions.
   b.   abstractions.
   c.   prototypes.
   d.   disjunctions

4.   The two most basic units of speech are:
   a.   syllables and rules of grammar.
   b.   ideas and concepts.
   c.   morphemes and phonemes.
   d.   connotative and denotative meaning.

5.   _____ are the smallest unit of speech.
   a.   Morphemes
   b.   Phonemes
   c.   Semantics
   d.   Syntax

6.   According to Noam Chomsky, we employ a set of rules to express ideas in a variety of way by applying:
   a.   functional rules.
   b.   generative rules.
   c.   semantic rules.
   d.   transformational rules.

7.   The inability to see new uses for familiar objects is termed:
   a.   inflexible thinking.
   b.   interference.
   c.   proactive.
   d.   functional fixedness.

8. Which of the following does not contribute to insight?
   a. selective attention
   b. selective encoding
   c. selective combination
   d. selective comparison

9. Computer programs capable of advanced knowledge of a specific skill or topic are associated with:
   a. proxemics.
   b. virtual reality.
   c. artificial intelligence.
   d. robotics.

10. The individual responsible for the development and design of the first intelligence test is:
    a. Freud.
    b. Terman.
    c. Binet.
    d. Wechsler.

11. The _____ intelligence test is composed of a set of increasingly difficult tests items for each age group.
    a. Terman's
    b. Stanford-Binet
    c. Wechsler's
    d. MMPI

12. Intelligence Quotient (IQ) may be defined as:
    a. MA/CA x 100
    b. CA/MA x 100
    c. CA X MA x 100
    d. MA/100 x CA

13. Jane has a mental age of 8 and a chronological age of 10; her IQ is:
    a. 100.
    b. 125.
    c. 80.
    d. 75.

14. A psychologist who wishes to assess a child's verbal intelligence and performance intelligence should use:
    a. WAIS-R.
    b. WISC-R.
    c. Stanford-Binet.
    d. Alphas test.

15. Thinking of many possibilities that are developed from one starting place is called:
    a. divergent thinking.
    b. convergent thinking.
    c. deductive reasoning.
    d. insightful thinking.

16. The dividing line between normal intelligence and retardation is an IQ of:
    a. 80.
    b. 70.
    c. 60.
    d. 50.

17. Familial retardation is associated with:
    a. genetic abnormalities.
    b. metabolic disorders.
    c. impoverished households.
    d. fetal damage.

18. Organic retardation can be caused by all of the following EXCEPT:
    a. genetic abnormalities
    b. poor emotional support
    c. fetal damage
    d. metabolic disorders

19. Tests developed so as to not disadvantage certain groups are called:
    a. culture-fair tests.
    b. counter-balance tests.
    c. Wechsler's tests.
    d. Alpha tests.

20. Thought that involves going from general principles to specific situations is called
    _____ reasoning.
    a. inductive
    b. divergent
    c. intuitive
    d. deductive

Chapter 9: Motivation and Emotion

1. The forces that act on or within an organism that initiate, direct, and sustain behavior as well as satisfying physiological or psychological needs are called:
    a.   drive.
    b.   instincts.
    c.   motivation.
    d.   homeostasis.

2. Which of the following is NOT a basic characteristic commonly associated with motivation?
    a.   activation
    b.   persistence
    c.   homeostasis
    d.   intensity

3. The tendency of the body to monitor and maintain internal states (like body temperature and energy supplies) at a relatively constant level refers to:
    a.   consistency.
    b.   homeostasis.
    c.   motivation.
    d.   incentive.

4. Emil is homeless and struggles to make money to feed and clothe himself. According to Maslow, Emil is attempting to meet his:
    a.   incentives needs.
    b.   physical needs.
    c.   self-actualization needs.
    d.   belongingness needs.

5. Motivation to eat is influenced by:
    a.   psychological factors.
    b.   biological factors.
    c.   environmental factors.
    d.   all of the above.

6. Jason's ventromedial hypothalamus (VH) was destroyed. This is most likely to:
    a.   increase his glucose levels.
    b.   decrease his insulin levels.
    c.   cause Jason to eat until he becomes obese.
    d.   cause Jason to stop eating.

7.   The hormone secreted by the pancreas that helps regulate the metabolism of carbohydrates, fats and starches in the body is:
   a.   serotonin.
   b.   endorphins.
   c.   insulin.
   d.   cholecystokinin.

8.   The excess fuel that our bodies do not use is:
   a.   metabolized.
   b.   used to produced insulin.
   c.   converted into fat.
   d.   stored in the pancreas.

9.   The particular weight that is set and maintained by increases or decrease in the metabolic rate is called:
   a.   homeostasis.
   b.   basal point weight.
   c.   set point weight.
   d.   drive reduction weight.

10.   The view that people are motivated to maintain a level of arousal that is neither too high nor too low is called:
   a.   arousal theory.
   b.   James Lange theory.
   c.   Cannon-Bard theory.
   d.   cognitive theory.

11.   A distinct psychological state that involves a personal experience, physical arousal, and a behavioral expression or response is known as:
   a.   motivation.
   b.   imitation.
   c.   self-actualization.
   d.   mood.

12.   The theory that emotions arise from the perception and interpretation of bodily changes is called the_____ theory of emotion.
   a.   James-Lange
   b.   Cannon-Bard
   c.   two-factor
   d.   facial-feedback

13. According to the _____ theory, the subjective experience of an emotion occurs simultaneously with physiological arousal.
    a. two-factor
    b. James-Lange
    c. Cannon-Bard
    d. cognitive

14. The notion that emotions can help or hinder performance is key to the:
    a. Schachter theory.
    b. Cannon-Bard theory.
    c. James-Lange theory.
    d. Yerkes-Dodson theory.

15. Frank and David fell madly in love and were prevented from marrying each other because it's illegal. It appears that they are:
    a. homosexual.
    b. bisexual.
    c. heterosexual.
    d. transvestites.

16. Jane is sexually attracted only to members of her own sex. Jane is a:
    a. bisexual.
    b. homosexual.
    c. heterosexual.
    d. transsexual.

17. Martina is sexually attracted to both women and men. By definition Martina is a:
    a. bisexual.
    b. homosexual.
    c. heterosexual.
    d. transsexual.

18. The first phase of the human sexual response cycle is called:
    a. plateau.
    b. excitement.
    c. organism.
    d. resolution.

19. _____ motivation influences us to engage in behaviors that are personally rewarding.
    a. Intrinsic
    b. Extrinsic
    c. Instinctive
    d. Attribution

20. Which sex-research pioneers first mapped the human sexual response cycle?
    a.   Ben and Lazarus
    b.   Cannon and Bard
    c.   Johnson and Johnson
    d.   Masters and Johnson

Chapter 10: Personality

1. Excessive concern with cleanliness and order could indicate a fixation at the _____ stage.
    a.   oral
    b.   anal
    c.   phallic
    d.   genital

2. When a young boy develops sexual feelings toward his mother and disgust toward his father, Freud would say the he has a conflict at the _____ psychosexual stage.
    a.   anal
    b.   genital
    c.   phallic
    d.   oral

3. Which of the following represents a primary source of influence on personality according to Freud?
    a.   heredity
    b.   adulthood
    c.   the strength of the id, ego, and superego
    d.   gender identity

4. According to Allport, the kind of trait that is a defining characteristic of one's personality is a _____trait.
    a.   common
    b.   source
    c.   secondary
    d.   cardinal

5. The two parts of the psyche that operate on all three levels of awareness are the:
    a.   id and ego.
    b.   id and superego.
    c.   ego and superego.
    d.   id and ego ideal.

6. Maslow used the term _____ to describe the tendency to make full use of personal potentials.
    a.   ego-idealization
    b.   self-actualization
    c.   self-potentiation
    d.   full functionality

7. The terms structured and unstructured apply most to:
   a. halo effect.
   b. interviews.
   c. questionnaires.
   d. honesty test.

8. The four types of temperament recognized by the early Greeks are melancholic, choleric, phlegmatic and:
   a. sanguine.
   b. sardonic.
   c. sagacious.
   d. sagi harian.

9. Who claimed that we could best understand personality by assessing people on two major dimensions, extroversion and neurotics?
   a. Raymond Cattell
   b. Carl Jung
   c. Gordon Allport
   d. Hans Eysenck

10. Freud used the term _____ to refer to sexual energy or motivation.
    a. thanatos
    b. libido
    c. latent content
    d. manifest content

11. The most widely accepted trait theory today is called:
    a. 16 PF.
    b. five factor model of personality.
    c. determinism model.
    d. meet-analysis model.

12. Cattell used a statistical method called _____ to describe a number of personality traits.
    a. factor analysis
    b. meta-analysis
    c. archetypes
    d. aptitude tests

13. The trait theorist who believed that personality could be described in terms of sixteen personality traits is:
    a. Hans Eysenck.
    b. Albert Bandura.
    c. Raymond Cattell.
    d. Abraham Maslow.

14. Traits that are easy to determine from observable behaviors are called _____ traits.
    a. surface
    b. source
    c. self-efficacy
    d. cognitive

15. A _____ is formally defined as a relatively stable, enduring pattern of behavior.
    a. trait
    b. emotion
    c. attribute
    d. behavior

16. According to the _____ model of personality, personality can be defined in terms of five basic dimensions.
    a. psychoanalytic
    b. 16 PF
    c. five factor
    d. attribute

17. In which personality test will people respond to ambiguous situations or images by projecting their own inner thoughts onto the test material?
    a. trait tests
    b. projective tests
    c. achievement tests
    d. aptitude tests

18. The two most widely used projective tests are the:
    a. MMPI and CPI.
    b. Rorschach inkblot and the Thematic Apperception test.
    c. 16 PF and Rorschach inkblot test.
    d. MMPI and Rorschach inkblot test.

19. In which test does the individual respond to specific questions and then compare their responses to established norms?
    a. projective test
    b. self-report inventory
    c. aptitude test
    d. achievement test

20. The most widely used self report inventory is called the:
    a. Thematic Apperception test.
    b. Rorschach inkblot test.
    c. Children's Apperception test.
    d. Minnesota Multiphasic Personality Inventory.

Chapter 11: Health, Stress, and Coping

1.   Real physical symptoms that are caused by psychological factors are called:
      a.   hypochondriac delusions.
      b.   prolonged stress.
      c.   psychosomatic symptoms.
      d.   schizophrenia.

2.   The little stressors that include irritating demands that can occur daily are known as:
      a.   hassles.
      b.   trials.
      c.   hang-ups.
      b.   major life events.

3.   We experience _____ when we are blocked from attainment of a goal.
      a.   frustration
      b.   anxiety
      c.   major life events
      d.   hang-ups

4.   Most researchers have pursued the connection between Type A behavior personality and:
      a.   cancer.
      b.   stroke.
      c.   obesity.
      d.   heart disease.

5.   Research suggests that the most toxic element of the Type A personality is:
      a.   hostility.
      b.   sense of urgency.
      c.   impatience.
      d.   perfectionism.

6.   Terrifying flashbacks, prolonged and severe stress reactions due to a catastrophic event or stressors is known as:
      a.   conflict.
      b.   frustration.
      a.   burnout.
      d.   post-traumatic stress disorder.

7. A person who is normally relaxed, easygoing, and has an optimistic approach to life is known as a _____ personality.
    a. Type B
    b. Type A
    c. introverted
    d. neurotic

8. According to Holmes and Rahne, the basic cause of stress is:
    a. divorce.
    b. depression.
    c. change.
    d. hassles.

9. The Social Readjustment Rating Scale measures:
    a. stress.
    b. hassles.
    c. life events.
    d. development.

10. Which of the following types of conflict produces the highest levels of stress?
    a. approach-approach conflicts
    b. approach-avoidance conflicts
    c. avoidance-avoidance conflicts
    d. all of the above

11. When a person feels torn between two or more opposing forces, the situation is referred to as:
    a. adaptation.
    b. conflict.
    c. hassle.
    d. resistance.

12. Laura is trying to lose weight and her friends are trying to tempt her with her favorite chocolate bar. She is torn between the candy and salad. Laura is experiencing an _____ conflict:
    a. approach-avoidance
    b. avoidance-avoidance
    c. approach-approach
    d. approach-escape

13. The _____ response to stressful situations results in a chain of internal physical reactions to prepare for the threat.
    a. startle reflex
    b. moro
    c. flight or flight
    d. escape-avoidance

14. Dr. Bernard studies the relationship between psychological processes, nervous and endocrine system functions and the immune system. What is her field?
    a. endocrinology
    b. behavioral medicine
    c. neuropsycholgy
    d. physiology

15. An _____ conflict involves choosing between two unappealing or undesirable outcomes.
    a. approach-approach
    b. approach-avoidance
    c. avoidance-avoidance
    d. escape-avoidance

16. The _____ is Hans Selyve's term for the three-stage progression of physical changes that occur when an organism is exposed to intense and prolonged stress.
    a. TAT
    b. GAS
    c. SRRS
    d. MMPI

17. During the _____ stage of the general adaptation syndrome, the symptoms of the alarm stage reappear, but this time irreversibly. The body's energy reserves are depleted, and adaptation begins to break down, leading to physical disorders or death.
    a. alarm
    b. exhaustion
    c. resistance
    d. plateau

18. Escape-avoidance is a(n) _____ coping strategy in which the person shifts his/her attention away from the stressors and toward other activities.
    a. emotion-focused
    b. problem-focused
    c. stress-focused
    d. immune-focused

19. _____ is a virus which enters the bloodstream through exchange of bodily fluids, primarily semen blood and blood products, and which may lead to AIDS.
    a. Gonorrhea
    b. HIV
    c. HPV
    d. Chlamydia

20. Stress reactions are most likely to occur when a stressor is viewed as a _____ during the:
    a. pressure; primary appraisal.
    b. pressure; secondary appraisal.
    c. threat; primary appraisal.
    d. threat; secondary appraisal.

Chapter 12: Psychological Disorders

1.   The term _____ refers to the study of the origins, symptoms and development of psychological disorders.
       a.   comorbidity
       b.   psychopathology
       c.   schizophrenia
       d.   psychosis

2.   Julie is excessively preoccupied with her children, her health, the bills and her job, even though there is no concrete reason for it. It appears Julie suffering from _____ disorder.
       a.   obsessive-compulsive
       b.   generalized anxiety
       c.   agoraphobia
       d.   panic

3.   Rene repeatedly checks his doors, windows and appliances before he goes to work. Rene is suffering from _____ disorder.
       a.   generalized anxiety
       b.   panic
       c.   obsessive-compulsive
       d.   phobic

4.   Edna has been housebound for 6 years. It appears that she is suffering from _____ disorder.
       a.   agoraphobia
       b.   claustrophobia
       c.   obsessive-compulsive
       d.   generalized anxiety

5.   After being attacked by a dog six years ago, Sean now gets hysterical whenever a dog approaches him. Sean is suffering from:
       a.   panic disorder.
       b.   generalized anxiety disorder.
       c.   social phobia.
       d.   specific phobia.

6.   Philip has extreme anxiety attacks that are incapacitating and come to him suddenly. Philip suffers from:
       a.   social disorders.
       b.   specific disorders.
       c.   generalized anxiety.
       d.   panic disorder.

7. Peter shows _____, because he laughs when at a funeral and cries when he hears a joke.
   a. delusions of grandeur
   b. hallucinations
   c. inappropriate affect
   d. delusions of persecution

8. Marco has several symptoms of being schizophrenic but does not fit any one disorder. Marco is a(n):
   a. paranoid schizophrenic.
   b. disorganized schizophrenic.
   c. catatonic schizophrenic.
   d. undifferentiated schizophrenic.

9. Peter stands in the same strange distorted position for long periods of time. Peter has been diagnosed as _____ schizophrenic.
   a. catatonic
   b. disorganized
   c. undifferentiated
   d. paranoid

10. Joe believes that aliens sent here to steal brain cells are in our midst. He believes they will bully him because he is the only one aware of their presence. Joe suffers from:
    a. delusions of grandeur.
    b. delusions of persecution.
    c. hallucinations.
    b. inappropriate affect.

11. There is substantial research that links the causes of schizophrenia with all of the following EXCEPT:
    a. genetic factors.
    b. extreme stress prenatally and postnatally.
    c. excessive dopamine activity.
    d. unhealthy family interactions.

12. Carlos has periods in which he is extremely depressed and becomes suicidal. At other times he appears jubilant and euphoric. He was diagnosed with:
    a. seasonal mood disorder.
    b. bipolar disorder.
    c. major depression disorder.
    d. dysthymia.

13. Jason lies, cheats, and exploits others without remorse. His behavior fits _____ personality disorder.
    a. avoidant
    b. narcissistic
    c. antisocial
    c. histrionic

14. _____ is a disorder in which an individual has sexual urges, fantasies and behaviors involving children, non-consenting partner or objects.
    a. Sexual dysfunction
    b. Homosexuality
    c. Paraphilia
    d. Voyeurism

15. _____ hallucinations are the most common type of hallucination experienced during a schizophrenic episode.
    a. Visual
    b. Auditory
    c. Taste
    d. Physical

16. Persistent, recurring thoughts are _____, while persistent urges to perform certain actions are:
    a. compulsions; obsessions.
    b. delusions; hallucination.
    c. obsessions; compulsions.
    d. hallucinations; delusions.

17. The basic idea behind the _____ hypothesis is that schizophrenia is caused by and increased brain activity of the neurotransmitter dopamine.
    a. serotonin
    b. dopamine
    c. acetycholine
    d. norepinephrine

18. _____ disorder is characterized by having two or more distinct, alternate personalities, each with its own name, history or self-image.
    a. Dissociative identity
    b. Disorganized identity
    c. Hebephrenic identity
    d. Paranoid identity

19. Taylene avoids getting to close to anyone because she fears they are out to get her and will use any information they find against her. Taylene is displaying _____ disorder.
    a. psychopath
    b. borderline personality
    c. paranoid personality
    d. dissociative personality

20. Bob has no memory of his actual identify or previous life. He believes his name is Elliot and he has always been a chef. Bob appears to have _____ disorder.
    a. dissociative amnesia
    b. dissociative fugue
    c. dissociative identity
    d. schizophrenia

Chapter 13: Therapies

1. The participant may imagine or experience painful or sickening stimuli associated with the undesirable behavior in:
   a. flooding.
   b. systematic desensitization.
   c. modeling.
   d. aversion therapy.

2. The client is taught progressive relaxation and is gradually exposed to the fear-evoking object during:
   a. flooding.
   b. aversion therapy.
   c. systematic desensitization.
   d. modeling.

3. For which disorder is ECT typically used?
   a. severe depression
   b. schizophrenia
   c. anxiety disorders
   a. panic disorders

4. To help promote self-directed change in the client, a _____ therapist strives to display genuineness, unconditional positive regard and empathetic understanding.
   a. Gestalt
   b. cognitive
   c. client-centered
   d. psychoanalytic

5. The use of psychological techniques to treat psychological problems is known as:
   a. psychoanalysis.
   b. biomedical therapy.
   c. psychotherapy.
   d. clinical psychology.

6. The primary goal of _____ is to bring unconscious conflicts to conscious awareness to help the client gain insight into conflicts and resolve them.
   a. Gestalt therapy
   b. psychoanalysis
   c. cognitive therapy
   d. client-centered therapy

7. Erica's therapist used a psychoanalytic technique in which she has told her to relax and to say whatever thoughts or images came to mind. The therapist was using:
   a. transference.
   b. free association.
   c. counter-transference.
   d. interpretation.

8. The disguised, hidden meaning of a dream is known as the _____ content from the traditional psychoanalysis perspective.
   a. manifest
   b. latent
   c. directive
   d. non-directive

9. The term _____ refers to the patient's unconscious attempt to block the revelation of repressed memories and conflicts.
   a. insight
   b. resistance
   c. transference
   d. latent content

10. The focus of _____ therapy is unlearning maladaptive behaviors and acquiring adaptive behaviors.
    a. behavior
    b. cognitive
    c. psychoanalytic
    d. Gestalt

11. The term _____ refers to computer generated scenes that a person views using a special motion censored helmet.
    a. cognitive reality
    b. network therapy
    c. MRI
    d. virtual reality

12. According to Albert Ellis, psychological problems are due to:
    a. conditional positive regard.
    b. unconscious innovations.
    c. modeling.
    d. irrational expectations and beliefs.

13. In _____ therapy, the therapist is non-directive, and uses unconditional positive regard and empathetic understanding to deal with life's difficulties and problems.
    a. cognitive
    b. rational-emotive
    c. behavior
    d. client-centered

14. The term _____ refers to the improvement of symptoms that sometimes occurs simply over the passage of time.
    a. spontaneous recovery
    b. spontaneous remission
    c. generalization
    d. extinction

15. The term _____ refers to a movement disorder characterized by severe, uncontrollable facial ties and grimaces and other involuntary movements.
    a. schizophrenia
    b. tardive dyskinesia
    c. extreme anxiety
    d. major depression

16. Risperdal and clozariol are both used to treat symptoms associated with:
    a. depression.
    b. anxiety.
    c. eating disorders.
    d. schizophrenia.

17. Two successful forms of cognitive therapy are:
    a. group and family therapy.
    b. national emotive and cognitive therapy.
    c. cognitive and humanistic therapy.
    d. psychoanalytic and rational emotive therapy.

18. Which of the following is NOT a humanistic therapy?
    a. client-centered
    b. Gestalt
    c. existential
    d. cognitive

19. Which of the following is a self-management technique?
    a. thought stopping
    b. REBT
    c. EMDR
    d. vicarious reality exposure

20.   Which technique most closely relates to the idea of non-directive therapy?
  a.   confrontation
  b.   dream analysis
  c.   role reversal
  d.   reflection

Chapter 14: Social Behavior

1.   The term _____ psychology refers to how the actual, imagined or implied presence of others affects our thoughts, feelings and behavior.
   a.   cognitive
   b.   social
   c.   biological
   d.   behavioral

2.   We tend to make _____ attributions to explain our own behavior.
   a.   situational
   b.   dispositional
   c.   proximal
   d.   cognitive

3.   We tend to make _____ attributions to explain the behavior of others.
   a.   situational
   b.   dispositional
   c.   proximal
   d.   cognitive

4.   The tendency of people to overemphasize dispositional causes and underemphasize situational causes when they explain the behavior of others is called:
   a.   false accusations.
   b.   self-selection bias.
   c.   fundamental attribution error.
   d.   external error.

5.   Antoine was initially asked to put a huge candidate's sign on his front lawn. When he refused they asked to place a smaller sign, to which he agreed. The technique they used is called _____ technique.
   a.   door-in-the-face
   b.   low-ball
   c.   foot-in-the-door
   d.   comparison

6.   What percentage of the subjects in Milgram's obedience experiment administered the maximum 450-volt shock?
   a.   85 percent
   b.   65 percent
   c.   45 percent
   d.   25 percent

7.   Rochelle agrees to baby-sit her neighbors' children, but when she arrived they told her their three nieces would be under her care also. The _____ technique was employed.
      a.   door-in-the-face
      b.   low-ball
      c.   foot-in-the-door
      d.   deception

8.   _____ occurs when members of gangs are more concerned with preserving the group solidarity than with challenging or evaluating possible solutions.
      a.   Group think
      b.   Group cohesiveness
      c.   Social facilitation
      d.   Group polarization

9.   _____ is a deliberate attempt to influence the attitudes and/or behavior of others.
      a.   Prejudice
      b.   Control
      c.   Persuasion
      d.   Discrimination

10.   Which of the following is NOT one of the components of an attitude?
      a.   emotional component
      b.   action component
      c.   behavioral component
      d.   belief component

11.   All of the following reduce cognitive dissonance EXCEPT:
      a.   changing attitudes
      b.   changing behavior
      c.   rationalizing the inconsistency
      d.   strengthening the attitude or behavior

12.   Kitt's salary is $600 less than John's, her male counterpart, even though their qualifications are the same. This is an example of:
      a.   stereotype thinking.
      b.   reverse discrimination.
      c.   prejudice.
      d.   discrimination.

13.   Bill can't stand Jews and refuses to allow any to move into his neighborhood. Bill's behavior is an example of:
      a.   discrimination.
      b.   prejudice.
      c.   stereotype.
      d.   tokenism.

14. According to the frustration aggression hypothesis, frustration _____ leads to aggressions.
    a. always
    b. sometimes
    c. never
    d. often

15. The _____ theory of aggression emphasizes when aggressive responses are reinforced, they are more likely to be continued.
    a. cognitive
    b. humanistic
    c. psychoanalytic
    d. social learning

16. The more people are present, the less likely it is that each individual is willing to help someone in distress. This is called:
    a. deindividuation
    b. social facilitation
    c. antisocial behavior
    d. bystander effect

17. A young woman's car breaks down on a busy highway and she is visibly in distress. Nobody stops to assist her. One explanation is:
    a. social facilitation.
    b. diffusion of responsibility.
    c. observer discrepancy.
    d. fundamental error.

18. The American social psychologist who is best know for his controversial study investigating destructive obedience to authority is:
    a. Solomon Asch.
    b. Stanley Milgram.
    c. Edward Tolman.
    d. Robert Beck.

19. The tendency to adjust one's behavior, attitudes, or beliefs to group norms in response to real or imagined group pressure is known as:
    a. obedience.
    b. conformity.
    c. facilitation.
    d. altruism.

20. The belief that one's own culture or ethnic group is superior to all others is a component of:
    a.   altruism.
    b.   centration.
    c.   collectivism.
    d.   ethnocentrism.

ANSWERS TO CHAPTER QUIZZES

Chapter 1: Psychology: The Search for Understanding

1. D	5. D	9. D	13. C	17. B
2. C	6. C	10. C	14. B	18. A
3. A	7. D	11. A	15. B	19. B
4. B	8. B	12. A	16. A	20. C

Chapter 2: The Brain and Behavior

1. A	5. C	9. D	13. D	17. C
2. B	6. A	10. C	14. B	18. B
3. C	7. D	11. A	15. C	19. B
4. B	8. B	12. A	16. B	20. A

Chapter 3: Human Development

1. B	5. A	9. C	13. C	17. C
2. C	6. A	10. C	14. B	18. B
3. B	7. D	11. D	15. A	19. B
4. D	8. B	12. B	16. B	20. B

Chapter 4: Sensation and Perception

1. B	5. A	9. A	13. A	17. A
2. A	6. B	10. B	14. B	18. D
3. B	7. D	11. D	15. C	19. C
4. B	8. C	12. B	16. B	20. B

Chapter 5: States of Consciousness

1. B	5. C	9. D	13. C	17. A
2. C	6. D	10. D	14. B	18. D
3. B	7. D	11. A	15. B	19. D
4. D	8. A	12. C	16. D	20. D

Chapter 6: Conditioning and Learning

1. C	5. C	9. C	13. B	17. C
2. C	6. B	10. D	14. A	18. D
3. A	7. A	11. A	15. A	19. B
4. A	8. B	12. C	16. C	20. C

Chapter 7: Memory

1. A	5. A	9. B	13. C	17. C
2. C	6. C	10. B	14. C	18. A
3. A	7. D	11. C	15. D	19. D
4. B	8. C	12. C	16. A	20. B

Chapter 8: Cognition, Intelligence and Creativity

1. A	5. A	9. C	13. C	17. C
2. C	6. D	10. C	14. B	18. B
3. C	7. D	11. B	15. A	19. A
4. C	8. A	12. A	16. B	20. D

Chapter 9: Motivation and Emotion

1. C	5. D	9. C	13. C	17. A
2. C	6. C	10. A	14. D	18. B
3. B	7. C	11. B	15. A	19. A
4. B	8. C	12. A	16. B	20. D

Chapter 10: Personality

1. B	5. C	9. D	13. C	17. B
2. C	6. B	10. B	14. A	18. B
3. C	7. B	11. B	15. A	19. B
4. D	8. A	12. A	16. C	20. D

Chapter 11: Health Stress and Coping

1. C	5. A	9. C	13. C	17. B
2. A	6. D	10. B	14. B	18. A
3. A	7. A	11. B	15. C	19. B
4. D	8. C	12. A	16. B	20. C

Chapter 12: Psychological Disorders

1. B	5. D	9. A	13. C	17. B
2. B	6. D	10. B	14. C	18. A
3. C	7. C	11. D	15. B	19. C
4. A	8. D	12. B	16. C	20. B

Chapter 13: Therapies

1. D	5. C	9. B	13. D	17. B
2. C	6. B	10. A	14. B	18. D
3. A	7. B	11. D	15. B	19. A
4. C	8. B	12. D	16. D	20. B

Chapter 14: Social Behavior

1. B	5. A	9. C	13. B	17. B
2. A	6. B	10. B	14. D	18. B
3. B	7. B	11. D	15. D	19. B
4. C	8. A	12. D	16. D	20. D